What Is It Doing?

A Book about Verbs

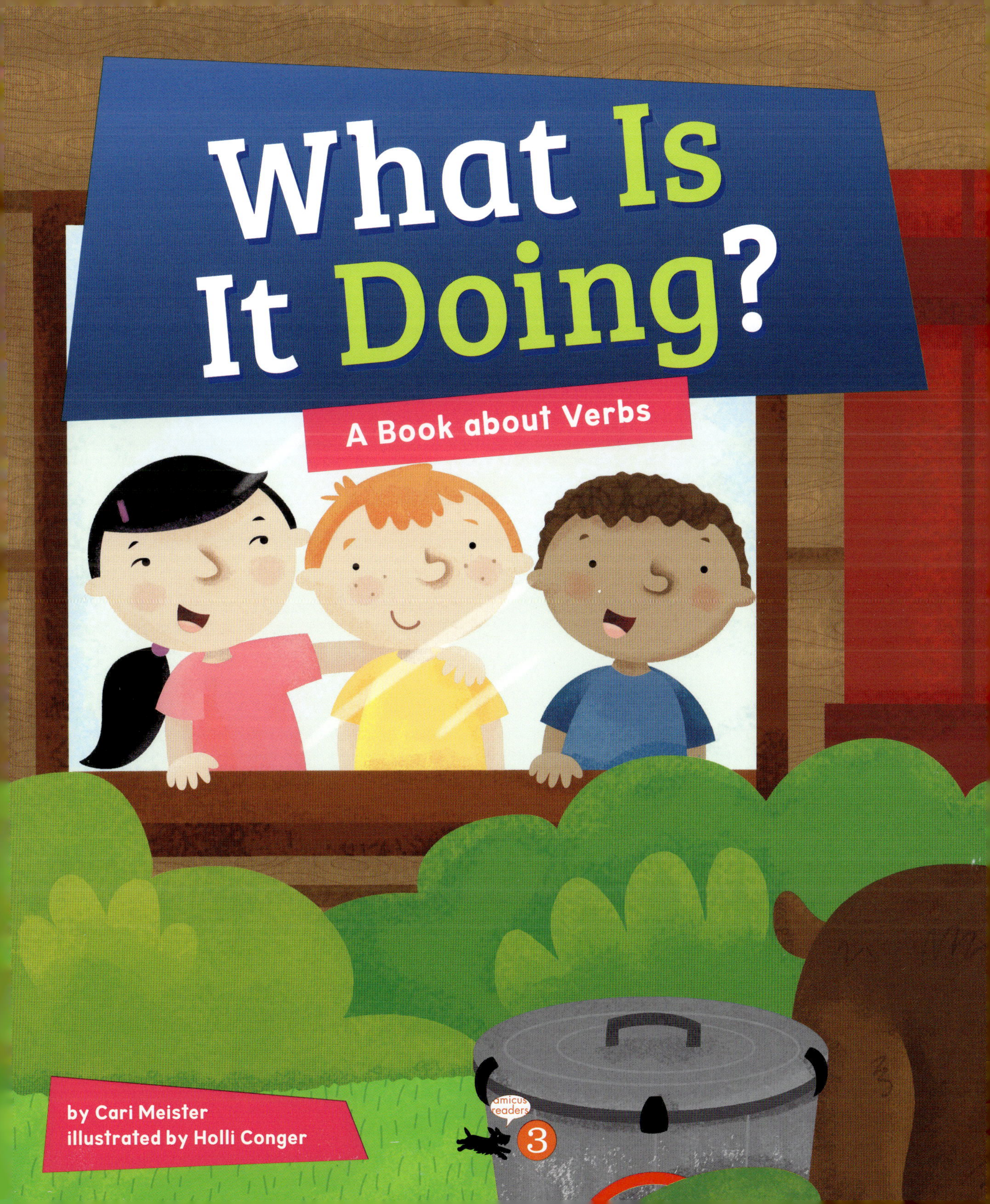

by Cari Meister
illustrated by Holli Conger

Say Hello to Amicus Readers.

You'll find our helpful dog, Amicus, chasing a ball—to let you know the reading level of a book.

1

Learn to Read

High frequency words and close photo-text matches introduce familiar topics and provide support for brand new readers.

2

Read Independently

Some repetition is mixed with varied sentence structures and a select amount of new vocabulary words are introduced with text and photo support.

3

Read to Know More

Interesting facts and engaging art and photos give fluent readers fun books both for reading practice and to learn about new topics.

Amicus Readers are published by Amicus
P.O. Box 1329, Mankato, MN 56002
www.amicuspublishing.us

Illustrations by Holli Conger
Editor Wendy Dieker
Designer Heather Dreisbach

Printed in the United States of America.

10 9 8 7 6 5 4 3 2 1

Library of Congress Cataloging-in-Publication Data
Names: Meister, Cari, author. | Conger, Holli, illustrator.
Title: What is it doing? : a book about verbs / by Cari Meister ; illustrated by Holli Conger.
Description: Mankato, Minnesota : Amicus, [2017]
Identifiers: LCCN 2015041492 (print) | LCCN 2015046776 (ebook) | ISBN 9781607539339 (library binding) | ISBN 9781681510576 (eBook)
Subjects: LCSH: English language--Verb--Juvenile literature. | English language--Parts of speech--Juvenile literature.
Classification: LCC PE1355 .M48 2017 (print) | LCC PE1355 (ebook) | DDC 428.2/4--dc23
LC record available at http://lccn.loc.gov/2015041492

A verb is an action word. It shows what people and things do. The purple words in the story are verbs.

Ping and William are sleeping over at Bernard's house. He lives in the woods.

“Do bears live around here?” asks Ping.

Bernard nods. “We see them all the time.”

William worries. He scans the yard. “Maybe we should go inside,” he says.

Early in the morning, the friends hear a crash.

"What is that?" asks William.

Bernard rolls over. "It is probably a bear. Today is garbage day. Bears always try to open the garbage bins."

Ping wrestles out of her sleeping bag. She dashes to the window. It is a bear!

William hides. “What is it doing?” he asks.

“It is turning this way!” says Ping.

"What is it doing now?" asks William.

"It is trying to open Bernard's trash can," says Ping.

"We have a bear-proof trash can," says Bernard. "The bear cannot open it."

BANG!
BANG!

“Look!” says Ping. “Now it is leaving.”

The three friends stare out the window.

“See, William,” says Bernard. “We are safe!”

Jobs of a Verb

Verbs have three main jobs.

Action verbs show what someone is doing.

William hides.

Linking verbs connect the subject of a sentence to information about the subject.

It is a bear!

Helping verbs work with a main verb. A common helping verb is is.

Now it is leaving.